WILDFLOWERS OF THE TOUR DU MONT BLANC

LESLIE MADSEN

"If you look the right way, you can see that the whole world is a garden."

– Frances Hodgson Burnett, The Secret Garden

NOTE FROM THE AUTHOR

As I was about to publish ***Wildflowers of the Tour du Mont Blanc***, the world shifted and life came to a halt. I had hoped that this book would be a useful tool as hikers geared up for another summer season of hiking the TMB.

As of early April, with countries around the world on lockdown due to the coronavirus, survival is front and center. Making plans for upcoming vacations vanished overnight as we all adapted to the new reality of quarantine and social distancing.

Confined at home, we are all communicating through virtual meetings, online learning platforms and other means. As we roll into spring and summer 2020, instead of being used as a field guide while hiking the Tour du Mont Blanc, perhaps this book (in various e-formats and paperback) can be used as a virtual tour of this very special trail.

Our feet may not be hiking the TMB for the foreseeable future but, if you have the time and inclination, maybe you can read these chapters and visualize yourself in a happy place, surrounded by meadows, mountains and, of course, incredible flowers.

Wildflowers are under a multitude of environmental pressures but they are hardy and resilient as well. Just like us. Stay strong and together we can weather this storm....

------Leslie Madsen

CONTENTS

PREFACE

As one of the most famous long-distance hikes in the world, the **Tour du Mont Blanc (TMB)** delivers the goods when it comes to fabulous scenery: massive mountains, impressive glaciers, endless vistas of valleys and the bucolic clanging of bells from bovines grazing in high meadow pastures.

Map of hiking the Tour du Mont Blanc

But *an overlooked bonus* of hiking the 105-mile TMB through France, Italy and Switzerland is *the smor-*

gasbord of colorful wildflowers whose histories are as fascinating as the flowers themselves are beautiful.

As a wildflower aficionado from Colorado, I was in hog heaven (yes, this is a real expression meaning "a state of complete happiness!") in early July of 2019 when I hiked the Tour du Mont Blanc. From the very first half-hour on the trail, I began to encounter a phenomenal amount of wildflowers that I didn't recognize from previous hiking trips in the U.S. and other countries.

For days, I would exclaim, "hey this flower must be in the bellflower family" or "wow, this orchid looks like the face of a ghost, I wonder what its name is!" This resulted in many ***hundreds of pictures of flowers that I did not know the names of***, an existential dilemma that made me crazy since I knew my beloved Colorado wild-flowers so well.

After several days on the TMB, tantalizing tidbits relating to flower identification began to emerge: a poster in our hotel in Courmayeur (see Chapter 4) and a small book in English also found in Courmayeur which identified a half dozen of the most common flowers. ***I was hooked!***

Upon my return to Colorado, my goal was to try and identify as many flowers as possible: a task that I presumed would be fairly simple but quickly morphed into an Alice-in-Wonderland-falling-down-the-rabbit-hole quest that required many months of research, the purchase of several books, hours of reading blogs on the internet and scouring plant apps for matches.

Having emerged from the rabbit hole, I am confident that the ***Wildflowers of the Tour du Mont Blanc*** is truly unique as there is no single source that documents the variety of wildflowers I found on my hike. It is my sincere hope that future TMB hikers will **find this book useful**

in real time as they sojourn through incredible land-scapes on their seven-to-fourteen-day hikes.

For example, while hiking the TMB you may come across a small, unassuming dark red flower and (while using this book as a guide) recognize it as a rare and protected Black Vanilla Orchid! Not only does this flower smell like vanilla and cocoa (don't miss out!) but after a long day's hike, you can entertain friends over beers at the bar by showing them your pictures while adding, "can you believe the locals used to tell tourists that cows who ate these flowers produced chocolate milk?"

And if you have already completed the ***Tour du Mont Blanc,*** perhaps you'll have an "aha moment" while reading this book as you discover that the ten-foot plant you stood next to for a photo included a Giant Yellow Gentian, a wildflower named for a king that lived two thousand years ago and is known far and wide for its medicinal (and alcoholic!) properties.

Lastly, if you have ever dreamed of hiking the Tour du Mont Blanc but it is not going to happen in the foreseeable future, then I hope you can turn the pages of this book and feel as if you are actually hiking the trail, witnessing these marvels of nature. For me, hiking is but the means to an end as **wildflowers are truly eye-candy for the soul!**

LES HOUCHES TO LES CONTAMINES

At 8:00 a.m. on July 6, 2019, my husband Paul and I caught the first tram on the Téléphériqué les Houches-Bellevue and thus embarked on an epic seven-day hike of the **Tour du Mont Blanc** (affectionately abbreviated by trekkers from around the world as the **TMB**).

As we wandered around looking for the trail variant we wanted to take, I was struck by multitudes of purplish blue-gray bellflowers, noteworthy for their perfectly shaped bells attached to a lovely, single green stalk. I was enamored with these flowers, not just because they were beautiful, but on closer inspection it was apparent that they were quite hairy.

Signage for Day One hiking on Tour du Mont Blanc

Bearded Bellflower (campanula barbata)

Yes, fine hairs covered the stems, stalks, leaves and bells, making the **_Bearded Bellflower (campanula barbata)_** a lovely addition to bucolic scenery that included the sound of cowbells tinkling in nearby pastures and snow-covered mountain peaks in the background. Oh, heavenly French Alps!

We hiked by several purple flowers of note that I'll describe later, but near the Mont Blanc Tramway sign (Gare de Bellevue Hiver) was another huge grouping of bellflowers, a variety that was not hairy, lol.

Scheuchzer's Bellflower (campanula scheuchzeri)

Prolific and attractive, we had just found a bunch of ***Scheuchzer's Bellflower (campanula scheuchzeri)***.

Our initial plan was to hike over the **Col de Tricot** but it was still too early in the season to attempt it; the route was still covered in snow. A big snow year also meant great wildflowers, so lucky us! Thus, for our first day on the TMB, we opted to hike the middle variant of the TMB (below the Col de Tricot but above the Col de Voza and Bionnasy).

Leaving the initial plateau behind, we descended down the trail and soon came across a hillside chock-a-block full of the most amazing lilies: the ***Martagon Lily (lilium martagon)***. This lily's deep color seemed to be a mixture of plum and mauve with a single, tall stalk measuring several feet, spouting multiple blooms.

Martagon Lily (lilium martagon)

Maybe magenta is the correct color for this lovely lily. The Martagon Lily can be found growing from Portugal to Mongolia, hence its origin is considered "Eurasian." Another name for the Martagon Lily is the "Turk's cap lily," presumably because the shape of the flowers curve upwards, resembling a turban.

In addition to the look of the lily, it is also noted that the word martagon might be traced back (middle English) to a Turkish word defined as some kind of turban. Lastly, do keep the cats you might be hiking with (lol!) away from this plant as apparently the pollen is highly toxic to our feline friends. As this lily has been domesticated and populates gardens in Europe and the U.S., the pet warning becomes more serious. A stunning flower in a stunning location…

As we continued downhill, the surprises just kept on rolling. In Colorado, I'm a big fan of our 28 native orchids, most of which are very difficult to find and are rarely found on hiking trails. I have tramped long and hard to locate and photograph the ones found in my state, and lo and behold, two of the prettiest orchids in the Alps just dotted the trail!

The lighter color orchid, the ***Common Spotted Orchid (dactylorhiza fushii),*** with its dense spikes of purple, pink or white flowers, seems to clown for the camera.

Common Spotted Orchid (dactylorhiza fushii)

A close-up of the Common Spotted Orchid reminded me of a laughing, whirling dervish. I decided that "delightful dervish" would be a good nickname.

And the nearby orchid, a deep purple variety, was an ***Early Purple Orchid (orchis mascula)*** which can be found all across Europe in a variety of habitats.

Early Purple Orchid (orchis mascula)

Both the Early Purple and Common Spotted orchids displayed distinctive spotted foliage (leaves at the base of the stalk). And get this: the Early Purple Orchid has been around and identified for a long time. More than one refer-

ence site stated the "long purple" in Shakespeare's Hamlet
was an orchis mascula. Here's an oft quoted line from
Queen Gertrude's Willow Speech (retelling Ophelia's
death):

*There with fantastic garlands did she come, of crow flowers, nettles,
daises and long purples, that liberal shepherds give a grosser name….*

I didn't know that hiking could be so educational!

We passed a stone cottage/residence of some sort (literally in the middle of nowhere) but with a number on it; a
directional sign across the road indicated we were at **Le
Planet.**

The cottage was
picturesque, surrounded by
planted, domesticated flowers.
Note in the accompanying
picture that the yellow, star-like
spikes (related to a hollyhock?)
make for an attractive garden
but is not part of the native
flora.

Continuing my quest to
locate more wildflowers, we
soon we came upon campions
similar to those found in

Stone Cottage at Le Planet

Colorado. The ***Alpine Red Campion (silene dioica)*** is
also known as a red catchfly in the States.

I just think it's a prolific, attractive, happy flower. We
ended up seeing a lot of this plant during the week. And
it's a member of the "pink" family, known technically as
Caryophyllaceae in Latin, which is both unpronounce-
able and impossible to memorize (duh!).

The white campion, or ***Bladder Campion (silene***

vulgaris), is native to Europe though it's also widespread in North America and is found in meadows and wooded areas.

I've found Bladder Campions on mountain biking trails in Winter Park and hiking in the Mt Evans State Wildlife Area (among other locations in Colorado). It's a very delicate and prolific wildflower that lends itself to great photos. If you look up this flower on Wikipedia, you'll see a bunch of references as to how the leaves are cooked and eaten in various countries, from Crete (in olive oil) to Italy (with risotto).

Alpine Red Campion (silene dioica)

A bridge led us over a river; we saw tons of additional orchids and I just couldn't resist taking more pictures, especially close-ups of that Early Purple Orchid.

Then I found a wildflower that resembled the plant I know as Prairie Smoke (geum triflorum); in Colorado it's a pink flower that is distinctively bowed down, or nodding as it's formally called. Later in the season when the Prairie Smoke goes to seed, it becomes a riot of candy-cane-like striped seed heads that sway in the wind.

Bladder Campion (silène vulgaris)

Today's wildflower had all the characteristics of a Prairie Smoke, yet the petals were shaped slightly different and the color appeared to be yellowish. Native to many parts of Europe, I had just found a **Water Avens (geum rivale)** and unfortunately, we never saw it again on the TMB.

Water Avens (geum rivale)

Even though we had only seen a few people in all the hours we had been on the trail, we came across a sign that tutored us on proper hiking etiquette; don't litter, don't let your dog chase the cows, keep fences closed and for heaven's sake, don't drive on the flowers!

Hiking Etiquette on the TMB

All sorts of interesting, historical signage now dotted the trail. All in French, naturellement, but the gist of each sign could be interpreted. Like when and how "le tramway du Mont-Blanc" was constructed, who settled in the area, how they could farm at such altitudes and what tools adventurers used such as crampons, batons and "la hache."

At the bottom of each descriptive sign was a trail map

of sorts that told you where, on this particular segment,

you were. Very interesting, indeed.

By the time we were around the #3 section, we saw this really cool bushy plant with spiky ends covered with delicate tiny white blossoms.

You Are Here Signage

Goatsbeard Spiraea (aruncus diocus)

The real name is **_Goatsbeard Spiraea (aruncus diocus)_** but is also known as bride's feathers; a perennial plant growing up to six feet tall, native to North America, Europe and Asia. As with many of the plants in this book, the roots of this plant have been used for medicinal purposes and it has been cultivated for domestic, garden purposes.

We decided on hiking one more variant before dropping into a few small towns and the long walk into Les Contamines where our hotel for the night was located. A steep trail led to groves of plants spouting three or more magnificent flower heads with 18+ spear shaped white petals (technically called bracts) that looked as if their tips had been dipped in green paint. Umbels of tightly packed, starry flowers burst from the center, appearing to be distinct flowers within a flower.

Great Masterwort (astrantia major)

Called a ***Great Masterwort (astrantia major)***, this wildflower is native to Europe and is part of the carrot family. I must have taken a hundred photos of this showy flower as it seemed to pose and change form depending on the angle of the picture. I could have spent ***hours*** meditating on its intricacy so I have knighted this wildflower as the ***Most Magnificent Masterwort***, Princess of the Alps!

Just to give you a flavor of traipsing from a wooded area to breaking out for miles of fabulous views and back into more woods is a panorama that captures the majesty of our first day on the TMB…

Panorma near Masterwort

Ever try to take a picture of a bee in focus?? My trash folder is full of out-of-focus wings and fuzzy bodies, but this picture of a ***Greater Knapweed (centaurea scabiosa)*** turned out great: the colors in the flower are so powerfully purple, highlighting the busy bees buzzing for their nectar reward!

It's always great to see which flowers attract which types of pollinators.

A ***Field Scabious (knautia arvensis)*** was nearby with a light purple, lovely flowerhead; its medicinal use included treatments of skin irritations including "sores caused by the bubonic plague."

Greater Knapweed (centaurea scabiosa)

Field Scabious (knautia arvensis)

And here's a beauty that I thought might be thistle of some sort until my botanist friend in Paris solved the riddle: it's a clover.

Red Trefoil (trifolium rubens)

Apparently, a common flower found in France, this **Red Trefoil (trifolium rubens)** was first classified by Carlos Linnaeus in 1753. It was difficult to find this flower in books or blogs so I consider it to be quite a unique specimen.

To wrap up describing the wildflowers we saw on our first day on the TMB, our last "find" involved a bushy plant with dozens of lovely white flowers, each sporting five heart-shaped petals. But it was the beetles that made these flowers so fascinating. They were **Spotted Longhorns** *(rutpela maculata)* that can be found in most of Europe, living for only 2-4 weeks. In addition to other pollinators (such as bees, butterflies, flies), certain wild-flowers depend on varieties of beetles for their reproductive future. I couldn't ascertain whether these Black and Yellow Longhorn beetles were mating or just crawling over one another in a frenzy to get to the nectar bar, but it was great to see the flower ecosystem in action!

Spotted Longhorns (rutpela maculata) Beetles

HIKING AROUND LES CHAPIEUX

Sidebar from the previous day: after a long but successful first day of hiking the TMB, we arrived at our hotel in **Les Contamines** to meet up with friends, enjoy malted beverages and dinner, then decide what to do about the weather forecast blowing in that night. It was early July and the following day we were supposed to hike over the **Col de la Croix du Bonhomme** to **Chapieux**; internet reports about this route always said "pray for good weather" when attempting this hike as there were no alternatives. There was still plenty of snow on the Col and the forecast was calling for storms throughout the next day.

The majority of our group decided to play it safe and hire vans that could drive us around to Les Chapieux in the morning. The new plan was for us to eat lunch in Chapieux and then day hike around the area. It's the hiker's yin/yang of guilt and relief, feeling like you've travelled many thousands of miles only to bail on a significant hike, yet not wanting to bite off more than you could chew (i.e. not having crampons, poles, etc. in case they were needed).

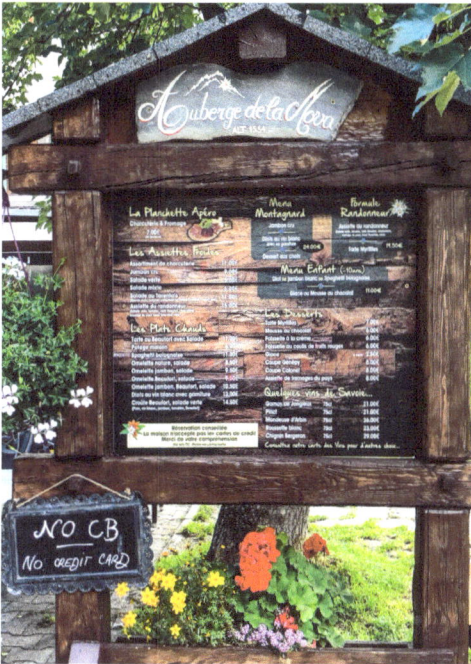

Refuge de la Nova

As it turned out, we were AMPLY rewarded for this decision, arriving at **Refuge de la Nova** via vans, stashing our packs, enjoying lunch, then day hiking an hour up the main TMB trail (where the Col du Bonhomme hikers would descend). We then deviated from the TMB, hiking a side trail that veered off east towards a lake past **Chalet du Petit Mont Blanc**.

Our first discovery above the village of Les Chapieux included giant stalks of yellow star-shaped flowers, six feet or more in height, happily populating the open hillside off the path. This is one of the most interesting wildflowers you will find on the TMB so it's worth memorizing a few factoids to remember as you encounter this colossal giant on your trek.

Great Yellow Gentian (gentiana lutea)

The **Great Yellow Gentian (gentiana lutea)** is native to central/southern European mountains and its stem is hollow and thick as a finger. Each stalk/stem can sport three to ten flowering clusters and get this: these plants may live for over 50 years! The Great Yellow Gentian is also known as "Bitter root" and is still used medicinally for many stomach and intestinal disorders. Historical lore has the plant named after King Gentius (second century BC) who discovered the healing properties of the gentian (reportedly an anti-malaria tonic as well).

Today, the Gentian root is still in demand as it is used to produce an iconic French aperitif named "Suze." Sold commercially since the 1800's, this alcoholic spirit even makes an appearance in a famous Pablo Picasso painting (La bouteille de Suze).

Hoary Plantain (plantago media)

Next up was a sighting of a ***Hoary Plantain (plantago media)***, a tall spiky flower with delicate, fragrant pink-white petals tipped with a whiteish anther (the male part that produces pollen). Apparently, this is a common plant, native to central and western Europe, but this is the only picture I have of a plantain during our entire hike.

I've just started noticing plantains in forest meadows around Colorado; I believe they are not native to the U.S. and were introduced at some point to North America. Not to be confused, of course, with the edible plantain in the banana family: totally unrelated plants!

Wig Knapweed (centaurea phrygia subsp. psedophrygia)

Another plant that looked like a tall flowering barrel cactus (from my untutored eyes) was actually a ***Wig Knapweed (centaurea phrygia subsp. psedophrygia***), related to the knapweed we saw the previous day. I believe it is native to Europe and has spread as far as Finland.

Bird's Foot Trefoil (lotus alpinus)

Not far away were clumps of bright yellow flowers called ***Bird's Foot Trefoil (lotus alpinus)***. They belong to an important family of flowering plants (legume, pea and bean). This trefoil is commonly found in mountain pastures in the Alps and Pyrenees and we were to see a lot of it over the coming few days.

Surprises popped up all around us as another yellow blazing star shaped flower with multiple anthers made an appearance. Google this flower, the ***Imperforate St. John's Wort (hyper-***

icum maculatum crantz), and watch reams of scholarly articles pop up on the "composition and antimicrobial activity of the essential oil hypericum maculatum crantz."

Yes, it's a beautiful flower but I'm nicknaming it "crazy crantz" for people's devotion to its medicinal properties!

We then passed by a triplet of **Common Hedgenettle (stachys officinalis)** which I thought for months might be a carnivorous butterwort but, NO, Hedgenettle is the correct identification.

Imperforate St. John's Wort (hypericum maculatum crantz)

Common Hedgenettle (stachys officinalis)

In French (and we were still in France!), its common name is bétoine but is also known as purple betony or bishopwort. Purple blooms sit on upright stems and the leaves are "toothed" and quite hairy. This wildflower has been written about for *thousands of years*, including an essay written by Antonius Musa (physician to Emperor Augustus, 63 BC to 14 AD) that extolled betony for its power to cure 47 diseases. If you're looking for a great flower with a fascinating medicinal and folklore history, spend some time on the internet as there are scholarly articles on the betony.

We hiked past the omnipresent Scheuchzer's Bellflower and soon came to wide open fields of very tall ***Dark Rampion (phyteuma ovatum)***.

Dark Rampion (phyteuma ovatum)

Native to the mountains of central and southern Europe, this flower is (surprisingly) a member of the **Campanulaceae** (bellflower) family. Spiky and stately, this was a beautiful grouping to behold.

Ironically, I got cut off from my hiking friends while I was busy snapping pictures of one of my favorite pink flowers, the ***Common Sainfoin (onobrychis vicifolia)***. This is a plant that animals (cattle, sheep, goats) love to eat and is supposedly good for them (i.e. anti-parasitic).

Common Sainfoin (onobrychis vicifolia)

A woman was repurposing an animal fence as I was taking this picture and she inadvertently captured me in the confines of the fence: I had to clamber over it to escape! We have pink sainfoin in open woodland locations in Colorado that I see occasionally; I'm always impressed by the sainfoin's distinctive veined, white/pink petals that seem to shoot upwards towards the sky.

Self-Heal (prunella vulgaris)

The next flower just knocked my socks off at first glance. The **Self-Heal (prunella vulgaris)** is a very famous wildflower that is known ***worldwide*** for its extensive medicinal properties; lol, it's even sold as a tincture for dogs. And yes, it's edible, even the stem and leaves. Native to Eurasia, it's now grown throughout North America in zones 4-9 (pretty damn hardy!).

We continued hiking through this amazing garden of never-ending flowers and noticed some bushy, lilac colored flowers on top of slim stems.

Matted Globularia (globularia cordifolia)

Matted Globularia (globularia cordifolia) is native to the central and southern mountains of Europe as well as western Turkey. Cordifolia plants are identified as having "leaves that are heart-shaped."

Panorama above Les Chapieux

We were well above the village now, taking in amazing views of the valley below and stopping to admire a prevalent wildflower found in open meadows: ***Golden Hawksbeard (crepis aurea)***. Not to be confused with dandelions, some references consider the Hawksbeard a weed, others suggest it is purposefully grown in pastures in Austria.

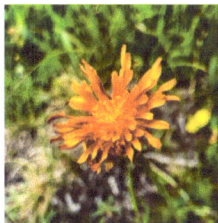

Golden Hawksbeard (crepis aurea)

And now we see another type of catchfly, this one a pinkish-white hue that apparently has a strong scent (to attract pollinators) and opens at night.

Nottingham Catchfly (silene nutans)

Called a ***Nottingham Catchfly (silene nutans)***, it's native to Europe but has been introduced to North America (where I've seen it on mountain hikes).

The trail got quite steep with switchbacks curving around rock formations resembling gardens. A prolific and fun plant was there to greet us: the ***Mountain Houseleek (sempervivum montanum)***, a very photogenic flower with pointed pinkish flowers and red-tipped basal rosettes.

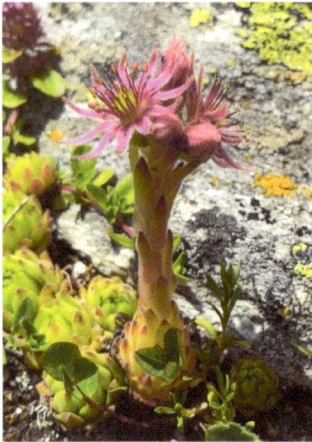

Mountain Houseleek (sempervivum montanum)

This hardy succulent is known as "hen and chicks" (as

the mother plant, hen, sends off numerous offshoots that gather around her base like "chicks"). The generic name sempervivum is derived from Latin (always living) because it grows in difficult conditions, including winters when it retains its leaves. The common name Houseleek comes from centuries ago when it was planted on the roofs of houses, ostensibly to protect them from storms, lightening and even sorcery!

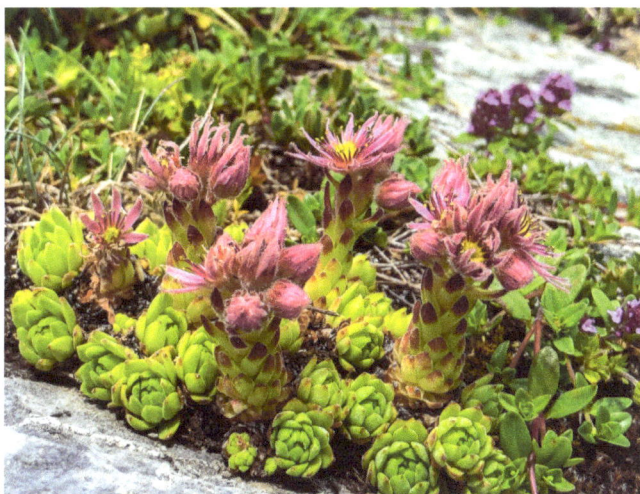

More Mountain Houseleeks in a natural rock garden

At this point, I've totally forgotten whatever guilt I had felt earlier in the day about bypassing the sketchy Col we were supposed to be hiking. Past the Houseleeks was an uncommon and very striking plant, a ***Yellow Bellflower (campanula thyrsoides)*** that boasts a flowering stem consisting of 50-200 tubular, bell-shaped, pale yellow flowers.

Yellow Bellflower (campanula thyrsoides)

It is protected in Germany, in parts of Austria and Switzerland (as well it should be). And even though it's considered a biennial plant that flowers and dies after two years, ***this wild Yellow Bellflower usually only flowers after eight years*** (or longer at higher altitudes).

So tread carefully, my friend, and if you come upon the Yellow Bellflower, recognize its importance in ecological perseverance. And as to who first documented this flower? Again, that mastermind and Swedish botanist, the father of modern taxonomy, Carl Linnaeus. **Existential hiker's dilemma**: are we just 21st century slackers, marching from hut to hut, not paying attention to the natural world around us? Centuries ago, Linnaeus was out cataloging thousands of plants and thinking deeply about the order of what grew and where. *Reflecting on the past can make us more mindful in the present.*

Just when I've thought that I've died and gone to flower heaven, it got even better….

Alpine Pasqueflower (pulsatilla alpine apiifolia)

We come to fields filled with one of my favorite flower characters of all time: a hippie-on-a-stick! Actually, it's an **Alpine Pasqueflower (pulsatilla alpine apiifolia)**, also known as an Alpine Anemone.

Alpine Pasqueflower (pulsatilla alpina apiifolia)

This wild wig of a plant gently swaying on its slender stem in the breeze is actually a flower that has gone to seed (i.e. a fruiting plant). This Pasqueflower is native to central European mountains and it looks quite different from its North American cousin (anemone occidentalis) that I have encountered in Canada and Oregon.

There are many subspecies of Alpine Pasqueflowers in the Alps and, quite frankly, it is difficult to tell them apart. The white flowers may be alpina alba, alpina baldensis or scherfelii…..whew! So, if my identifications are incorrect, just know that scholarly articles describing pulsatillas in great detail are easily found (in case you have insomnia).

My best guess is that this yellow flower and its corresponding seedheads represent the pulsatilla alpina apiifolia. Just saying!

BTW my husband's favorite flower in Colorado is an alpine forget-me-not that is found above timberline, usually on mountain summits around 12,000 feet. It's a cushion plant of sorts and sports miniature, delicate blue flowers. On this hike, we find another genus of forget-me-not, also called an **Alpine Forget-Me-Not (myosotis alpestris)** which is a beautiful specimen with sky blue petals and yellow centers.

Alpine Forget-Me-Not (myosotis alpestris)

This variety is also the state flower of Alaska whereas our Colorado high-altitude version is in the same plant family (borage) but is from an entirely different genus (eritrichium nanum). Myosotis means "mouse's ear" in ancient Greek but, for whatever reason, I don't really see the resemblance!

Last, but not least, was a distinctive, purplish plant stacked like a pyramid with a three-lobed-lipped flower emanating from the stem onto each individual leaf. The flowers can be blue, purple, whitish or pink.

Pyramidal Bugle (ajuga pyramidalis)

It was a hairy plant for sure; a ***Pyramidal Bugle (ajuga pyramidalis)*** can grow to 12" high and is a member of the mint family. Native to Europe, it seems to proliferate in different geographical locations from the Alps to Scotland and Finland. I've never seen anything like it in Colorado.

As we descended on the trail from an excellent afternoon of hiking and flower-hunting, we heard a faraway cry that almost sounded like an injured child. Looking up at the jumble of rocks, we picked out a herd of 12-15 ibex scrambling from one area to another. Including young ibex, they were masters of rock climbing. A very special treat to end a wonderful day.

Hidden Pictures: find the ibex!

LES CHAPIEUX - COL DE LA SEIGNE - COL DE CHAVANNES – COURMAYEUR

The best part of an abbreviated TMB hike is chopping off valley walks while still packing in plenty of miles, vertical, scenery, and of course, flowers!

Leaving the Refuge de la Nova in Les Chapieux, we took a bus to **Le Ville des Glaciers** and started off on a long day's hike. The first hour we gained altitude on a rocky road, hiking through a wide green, glacier valley dotted with a few stone cottages and great vistas. We were on the main TMB trail and trekkers from all over the world were headed toward the **Col de la Seigne**, a pass on the border of France and Italy that links the Chapieux valley from the southwest to the Val Vény (or Veni on my large map) to the northeast.

Towards the summit, the trail became much steeper but my husband and I were having a great time chatting with some of our best friends from California (I was also singing songs from various musicals, a preoccupation I have at higher altitudes!). Of course, I came to a dead halt as soon as I found a treasure trove of alpine beauties.

This hardy, bright pink *Least Primrose (primula*

minima) was a startling contrast to the well-worn, main TMB trail beside it.

Least Primrose (primula minima)

But perhaps Benjamin Maund described this flower best in his 1836 book entitled ***The Botanic Garden*** (from Great Britain). Maund states:

> *Every species of primula is met with pleasure. The whole family appear to be associated with the first-coming rays of Spring—the cheering sunbeams of April and May—green meadows, and universal gladness. Spring and primroses are the poet's own subjects, and from them we imbibe not a few of our pleasures.*

When hiking the TMB (or anywhere for that matter), take a moment and savor the ***flower power poetry*** around you!

Not far from the least primrose was a beautiful flower we had spotted the day before, though that specimen was barely open.

This ***Spring Gentian (gentiana verna)*** was in full bloom, producing an eye-popping vivid blue hue that was spectacular. While this gentian species may be a common flower in Eurasia, from Ireland to Russia, true blue flowers are a rarity in nature.

There were a lot of hikers milling around the summit of **Col de la Seigne** at 2,516 m (8,250 ft), taking selfies and admiring the views. From the Col, the main trail heads down valley towards Rifugio Elisabetta (where I presumed we'd have lunch).

Spring Gentian (gentiana verna)

But no, my husband and I left the hiking hordes behind and quickly veered off the main TMB to a SE variant path that hugged under Mont Lechaud (headed to the **Col de Chavannes**). Staying high, instead of descending, meant crossing snowfields. The drill was to just take it slow, dig in a platform with your hiking boots, and know how to self-arrest if for some reason you lose your footing.

The reward was virtually no people on this trail (i.e. who would be silly enough to traipse off into the snowy unknown) as well as new flowers waiting to be discovered.

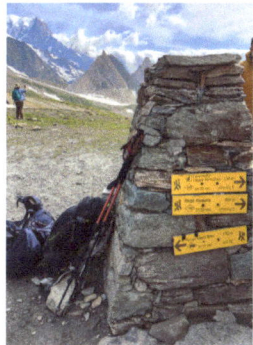

Col de la Seigne

Like this absolutely adorable ***Alpine Snowbell (soldanella alpina)***, a purplish, fringed wildflower that is fragile, delicate and native to the Alps.

The slender, woody-looking stems were sporting clusters of 2-3 flowers and the leaves were dark green and roundish.

Alpine Snowbell (soldanella alpina)

Unbeknownst to me, the four or five pictures I took of this little grove of snowbells was fortuitous as *we never saw them again anywhere on the TMB!*

And hiding amongst the rocks was a little cluster of **Yellow Whitlow-Grass (draba aizoides)**, a bright yellow beauty that actually took months to identify.

Yellow Whitlow-Grass (draba aizoides)

Common throughout central and southern European mountains, this flower is actually an alpine herb, a member of the **Brassicaceae** family that includes plants such as bok choy, broccoli and brussels sprouts.

Another rock-loving flower is the ***Glacier Crowfoot (ranunculus glacialis)***, also known appropriately as the glacier buttercup. I found more than one source that says it's the highest growing alpine flower, even found above 4,000 m (or 13,000 ft). Charming!

Glacier Crowfoot (ranunculus glacialis)

Gorgeous views of mountains down valley gave way to several other rock clinging wildflowers like this **Round-leaved Pennycress (noccaea rotundifolia**), crowded with dozens of lilac colored flowers punctuated by yellow centers.

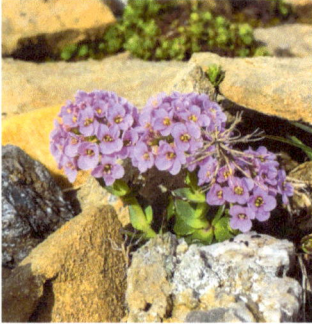

Round-leaved Pennycress (noccaea rotundifolia)

I originally identified this as an alpine rock jasmine but research pointed me in the pennycress direction. Truly a lovely, delicate clump of flowers that were breathtaking at altitude.

I was really proud of this next picture believing that I had found an Alpine Pasqueflower that was transforming from flower to seed; for days I showed it to anyone who would take the time to listen to me brag. Later, I determined it was actually a **Creeping Avens (geum reptans)** because of its "buttery yellow blooms" that soon give way to "fluffy pink seedheads." I gave myself brownie points for enthusiasm even when my veracity was in doubt!

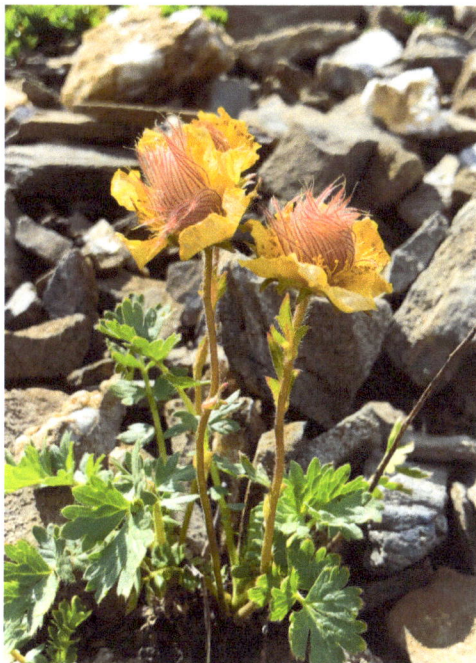

Creeping Avens (geum reptans)

There's nothing like finding a natural alpine rock garden, far above timberline (or bushline as our Australian mates call it), framed by an incredible mountain landscape. This one featured pink ***Moss Campion (silene acaulis)*** as well as more of the sky-blue Alpine Forget-Me-Nots. Moss Campion is a common plant throughout the northern arctic and high mountains of Europe and North America (in Colorado it is found well above timberline).

Alpine Rock Garden with Moss Campion (silene acaulis)

This alpine tundra plant faces harsh conditions (snow, wind, sub-freezing temperatures), hence they are ground hugging with buds tucked within the foliage for maximum protection. Once these buds pop, the plant explodes in a riotous pink cushion of delicate flowers. And, as Moss Campion is a slow grower, *never, EVER, step on one of these plants* as it can take decades for the plant to recover (and they can survive for 70-100 years!).

Even though this book is about the wildflowers of the TMB, a brief pause to explain a situation on this Day 3 hike that might not have ended well or could have ended prematurely (as in disaster!). After the rock garden, we came upon one last snowfield to cross. But this was not just a "take-your-time-crossing-this-snowfield," rather it was a black diamond ski run, 100 yards of treacherous, steep "you-make-one-mistake-and-you're-toast-in-the-rocks-500-feet-below" type of crossing.

What made it so frustrating is we could see where our trail emerged on the other side of the snowfield, knowing it would get us to the summit. But there was literally no way to circumnavigate this enormous snowfield: you had to either drop back down to the valley and abort the route or attempt a more-than-sketchy crossing.

We hadn't seen another soul for hours. But, as Paul and I were standing there debating what to do, I saw a guy hiking up the trail behind us. It would take him five or ten minutes to catch up, but he had poles and was definitely coming our way. I said, "well let's wait for him; maybe he'll have an idea!"

Long story short: our "snow angel's" name was Andreas and he was a solo hiker from Sweden.

Andreas, our "snow angel!"

He had originally planned on hiking the TMB with his girlfriend (bad idea?) but she bailed. Lucky us! Andreas had crampons and said he'd be glad to put them on and kick in a path for us to follow. It was slow going (Andreas, Paul, then me) and it was so steep that my right hand got super cold (even in a light weight ski glove) as it was permanently planted in the snow holding onto the "wall" next to me.

Andreas, we still owe you a beer if you ever read this story….

So, we made it to the **Col des Chavannes**, elevation 2,592 m (8,500 ft) and the views were absolutely stunning. Across the valley, wind was blowing snow off a peak and it looked exactly like a snowy volcanic eruption.

Col des Chavannes

I fished out a long-forgotten biscuit from my pack as we had no food and many miles to go….hopefully, we would not encounter additional snowfields. And lol, although there were no mountain bikers to be seen on this day (perhaps the snow kept them off our trail!), there was a numbered marker; months later I looked up this trail on a Red Bull mountain biking website that described it as "challenging, at times scarily exposed" and "not for the faint hearted." A marketing understatement perhaps?

Trumpet Gentian (gentiana acaulis)

Done with summits, we continued our hike, finding a patch of **Trumpet Gentian (gentiana acaulis)**, with (duh!) trumpet-shaped blue flowers, often without leaves (or one or two pairs). I thought at first that it could be a gentiana clusii that we had seen in Slovenia the previous summer. However, this gentian grew in a different soil type and also had telltale olive-green spots on the inside of its trumpet throat.

Panorama on TMB variant

We were now hiking through Italy with nary a soul in sight: this panorama demonstrates how perfect weather allows travelers to see for many miles in all directions. We passed more Spring Gentians and Kidney Vetch (described later) until we came across a very rare and unusual alpine wildflower.

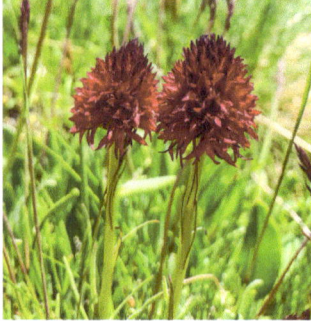

Black Vanilla Orchid (gymnadenia rhellicani)

Formerly known as nigritella nigra, the **Black Vanilla Orchid (gymnadenia rhellicani)** is a dark red, almost blackish European orchid that exudes a subtle chocolate scent.

Folklore has it that grazing cows who consumed these orchids produced chocolate milk, but I presume that most countries have similar silly sayings that are just as "udderly" ridiculous! Seriously, this is an endangered, protected plant and to see two black vanillas together was truly a special treat.

Down the trail we spotted a solo Yellow Bellflower that was not fully in bloom and continued hiking past a very pretty alpine lake with many clumps of bright blue Spring Gentians.

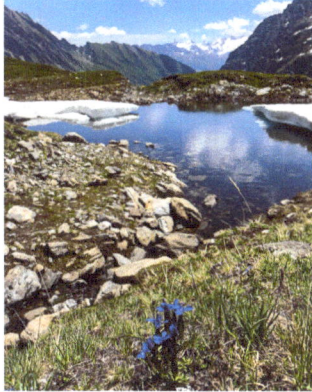

Alpine Lake and Spring Gentians

A new flower surprised us: the delicate ***Recurved Sandwort (minuartia recurva)*** that loves a sunny, rocky location. It sports five rounded, white petals with protruding light pink anthers.

Recurved Sandwort (minuartia recurva) on the trail

At first, I thought this was a mossy saxifrage but later

research showed it to be a member of the minuartia genus of flowering plants known as sandworts.

Recurved Sandwort (minuartia recurva) close-up

More **Mountain Thrift (armeria alpina)** wildflowers dotted the trail. This pinkish, purplish multi-bloom tuft is set atop a slender, hairless green stalk.

Mountain Thrift (armeria alpina)

In the flower-filled meadows we spied a couple of tall, white anemones that were spectacularly different than the smaller, yellow versions we saw the previous day. In all likelihood, these are true Alpine Pasqueflowers (pulsatilla alpina) but they appeared to be a different subspecies of pasqueflower, such as an anemone baldensis or possibly a pulsatilla scherfelii.

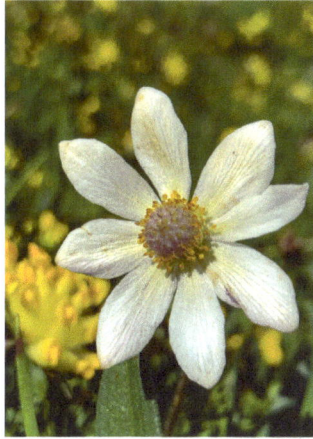

White Pasqueflower (pulsatilla vulgaris 'alba')

So now I'm going out on a limb and anointing this particular flower to be a ***White Pasqueflower (pulsatilla vulgaris 'alba')***. Why? Because even though the standard pulsatilla vuglaris is purple, it is native to Europe; the alba is just a white variety that is also characterized by solitary flowers that can grow 9-12" tall. I can only spend so many hours agonizing over these smallish details and then it's time to move on….

Next, we discovered a real treasure: not a Great Yellow Gentian, but another notable variety called a ***Spotted Gentian (gentiana puntata)***. At over two feet tall, it had clusters of upright bell-shaped flowers and large, cabbage looking leaves. Bonus flower find!

Spotted Gentian (gentiana puntata)

Then we reached a fork in the trail with two choices: either start hiking down valley (and hopefully catch the bus into town) or hike back up another trail to the top of a ski run for a steep three-mile bushwhack straight down into Courmayeur. Either way would take many hours. Andreas, the snow angel, had informed us that the chairlift we were expecting to take into town from the top of the ski run was not in operation until the following weekend. Whoops! So we opted for the first option, thinking it might be the quickest way out.

Not knowing what we missed on "the road not taken," our trail was lovely as it exploded with acres and acres of wild ***Alpenrose (rhododendron ferrugineum)***, a glorious evergreen shrub with clusters of pink to dark pink bell-shaped flowers.

Alpenrose (rhododendron ferrugineum)

The generic name rhododendron comes from the Greek rhodon or 'rose' and dendron or 'tree.' We had seen some Alpenrose on previous hikes but nothing compared to the ones we saw on this day as they intermingled with Mountain Milk-Vetch, Forget-Me-nots and other assorted flowers.

A notable yellow flower included in this meadow mix of prolific wildflowers was the ***Buckler Mustard (biscutella laevigata)***.

Buckler Mustard (biscutella laevigata)

Sprays of small yellow flowers sat atop tall green stems, quite a show stopper….the Buckler Mustard made a lovely complement to a bushel of Recurved Sandworts with a couple of Golden Hawksbeards tossed in for effect.

Descending towards the valley, we saw flowers that were now familiar to us such as Alpine Red Campion. A surprising new purple flower appeared, a **Wood Cranes-bill (geranium sylvaticum)**, native to Europe and northern Turkey.

According to that encyclopedia of sometimes-correct-information, Wikipedia states that these flowers yield a blue-gray dye that was "used in ancient Europe to dye war cloaks, believing it would protect them in battle." For this reason, it was called "Odin's Grace."

Wood Cranesbill (geranium sylvaticum)

Once on the valley floor, we walked along a defined path that was surrounded on both sides by huge, dark green leaves with spiky stems sporting clusters of purple flowers. ***Adenostyles (adenostyles alliariae)*** feature a unique arrangement of tiny tube flowers shaped like a ball; I'm sure these plants were beautiful later in July as the flowers opened up.

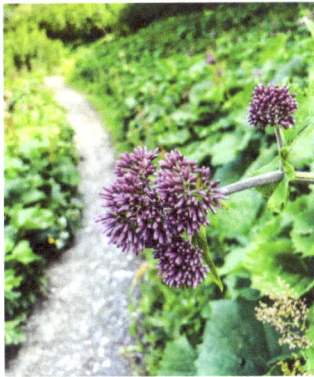

Adenostyles (adenostyles alliariae)

Rejoining the main TMB trail, we met another couple that also happened to live in Denver; as we walked with them towards the bus stop, I happily pointed out Mountain Houseleeks and Martagon Lilies that lined the road. Even walking at a brisk pace, we barely caught the bus in time as it only shows up once an hour, loads hikers and departs. After a long but scenic ride to **Courmayeur**, we got off the bus but had some difficulty finding our hotel as it was tucked away on a confusing side street. We didn't get to a restaurant until 20:00 hours and, after such a big day and no food on the trail, we were positively famished!

4

COURMAYEUR

After the previous day's huge hike, we were pleased to spend two nights and one day at a charming, comfortable family run hotel called the **Hotel Bouton d'Or** in **Courmayeur**. The hotel is named after a famous flower, the Bouton d'Or (globeflower), beloved in France and Italy.

I had to take a picture of the poster in the hotel lobby; hopefully it was a harbinger of flowers still to be seen as the next hiking segments would take us out of Italy, into Switzerland and back to France....

Poster of Bouton d'Or in hotel of same name

My goal for our 'down day' (besides enjoying a real café au lait) was to see more flowers and attempt to identify varieties we had found on the first half of the TMB. When we booked this trip, I was hoping to visit the **Sassurea Alpine Botanical Garden** outside of Courmayeur; I kept my fingers crossed that in early July the snow would have melted and that the flowers would be in bloom.

The purchase price of a ticket at the **Skyway Mont Blanc** station also covered the entrance fee for the alpine garden (it's a six-minute ride from the valley floor to the first stop, Pavillon du Mont Fréty, altitude 2,133 meters or 7,000 feet). Bonus: good weather down below provided great views from Val Veny, from where we came, to Val Ferret, our destination on the following day. Mont Blanc was shrouded in clouds that day and the skyway was crowded so I didn't feel compelled to go farther up (plus we had been to the Aiguille du Midi from Chamonix on a previous vacation).

The alpine garden is a short walk from the station exit;

there was an Italian guy checking tickets at the entrance and, without sounding like an ugly American, I was surprised that he did not speak English and that none of the literature or brochures were in English either (i.e. not good for their marketing efforts). However, he was selling really cool, little potted containers of ***Edelweiss (leontopodium nivale)***. Had I been at home, I would have gladly bought a bunch of them for my garden in the backyard.

The only Edelweiss I've found in the wild was, unfortunately, limp and wilted. In September, 2014, Paul and I were hiking in the Dolomites, up an incredibly steep route from Refugio Brogles to the top of the Forcella Pana. Looking down on Val Gardena we found a sad looking, past-its-prime, lonely little Edelweiss.

So I'm really quite proud of this Edelweiss picture from Courmayeur as it is a total optical illusion featuring potted flowers and part of the Mont Blanc massif in the background!

Cultivated Edelweiss (leontopodium nivale) at Sassurea Alpine Botanical Garden

The importance of botanical gardens cannot be over-stated: worldwide, they exist to protect, preserve, research and educate people about native plant species that are diminishing due to habitat encroachment and climate change. We need to support these gardens with our money, time and talent. Symbiotic ecosystems are disappearing right now, in our lifetime, and they are demanding our immediate attention. If you're mindful and live in the present, make sure you give something back to the environment you love....

Sassurea Alpine Garden

The **Sassurea Alpine Garden** was a pleasant way to walk amongst flowers we had already seen (like Mountain Thrift, Spring Gentians, Anemones, etc.) and to look at others we might encounter in the future. Unfortunately, a significant part of the garden was closed due to construction. Although no special events were available on the day we visited, the garden hosts a plethora of exciting activities from yoga to musical lectures so make sure you check their schedule when visiting.

Back in town, we wandered the streets, had lunch on an outside patio at some fun restaurant, then did a little souvenir shopping. I was looking for a book on wildflowers and found one, in English, at a bookstore in the center of Courmayeur. Published by Kompass, it is called ***Nature Guide*** and edited by Dr. Christine Jaitner. A yellow sticker on this small book's cover stated it contained "70 Alpine Flowers, 70+ photos" (of the most common and abundant alpine plants). FYI, as helpful as this book was, it contained only a dozen+ flowers that I've identified for this book. But it became my flower Bible and I thirsted for more photos, more info!

I had made a reservation months in advance for a romantic, expensive, sit-down dinner that night as an excuse to wear real clothes versus our usual hiking boots and garb.

Ristorante Pierre Alexis 1877

Ristorante Pierre Alexis 1877 is found in a quaint alley off the beaten path in Courmayeur and features local ingredients and chef inspired cuisine.

There was a tad of guilt that accompanied such a delightful and surprising meal: i.e. the reality that we were "glamping" the TMB versus doing a hard-core version! After days on the trail, how do you choose from appetizers that included *Fassona beef tartare* (snail and its caviar, veal soup, wild garlic air) or *Guinea fowl mousse with black truffle* (calvados apple sauce). I had a lovely first dish of Tortelli (description on menu: [36 egg yolks on 1 kg of flour] of creamed cod, sauce Norway lobster carapace, confit tomatoes, peas).

Tortelli at Ristorante Pierre Alexis 1877

And here's a mouth watering dessert, just one of two we ordered: a goat milk foam, cassis ice cream, blond dulcey chocolate, hazelnut crumble. What a fabulous dinner….

Goat milk foam dessert at Ristorante Pierre Alexis 1877

5

COURMAYEUR - GRAND COL FERRET - CHAMPEX

Rested, and more than well fed, we said goodbye to the friends in our group that were on the fourteen-day hike (our self-guided tour had them staying in Cour-mayeur for one more night, then not taking shortcuts back to Chamonix).

Today's agenda for the abbreviated TMB hikers involved two bus rides on each end, a morning ride through Val Ferret arriving at **Arnuva** (buy a ticket early in Courmayeur and stand in line at the correct bus stop) and another bus we'd have to track down much later in **Ferret**.

The first flower surprise of the morning was along a streambed. It was hard to get a decent picture of this flower because it was in deep shade, nonetheless, this spec-imen of ***Wolfsbane (aconitum lycoctonum)*** was spec-tacular.

Wolfsbane (aconitum lycoctonum)

It's also known as aconitum vulparia and is native to the Alps of central Europe. Growing two to three feet in height, the flowers are a lovely pale yellow yet be aware that the roots and sap are quite toxic. Odd then that Wolfsbane has been associated with werewolves and the ability to ward them off in some magic potion way. In Colorado, we have another member of the genus aconitum (aconitum napellis) which is commonly found at higher elevations. It's a deep purple and known as Monkshood; there's a European equivalent but, unfortunately, I haven't found one yet.

We gained altitude in our quest to ascend to the **Grand Col Ferret** at 2,537 m (8,323 ft).

And then, looking down the valley we had just hiked, a grove of fabulous, fantastic, bright yellow Bouton d'Or jumped out to meet us! The ***Globe-***

Trail to Grand Col Ferret

flower (trollius europaeus) is a waxy, glossy, golden and mostly closed flower that forms a spherical shape. Their straight stems can reach two feet in height and are held high with distinctive palm-like leaves.

Globeflower (trollius europaeus)

Another photographer conundrum: After months (post-trip) of trying to correctly identify (100%) the next flower we came across, I have given up! It's a yellow-orange butter-cup-looking flower on a sturdy stem with heart (or kidney) shaped leaves. I presumed it was an ***Alpine Avens (geum montanum)***; I'm now sticking with this original observation even though a French plant app gave me a 5-star match as Cowflock (caltha palustris L).

Alpine Avens (geum montanum)

Cowflock is extremely surprising since the other common name for that flower is marsh marigold. Other than melting snow and rainfall, this was not a boggy area. And a North American version of marsh marigold is one that I encounter frequently in wet, alpine environments in the Rocky Mountains. The habitat on the TMB suggested it was an Alpine Avens.

And then **the conundrum continued** with a nearby flower that was yellow and hairy.... My motivation for spending a lot of time on this book was to get it into the hands of TMB hikers so that they could identify wild-flowers in **real time**. I mean really....who wants to return home after a vacation and spends months looking at websites, plant apps and books on wildflowers in Europe?

Finishing this book was supposed to remove the ambi-guity of flower identification found on the TMB. Now I've come to realize *this quest is but a larger metaphor for living life*: eliminating uncertainty is not possible. It's how we deal with the uncertainty that's important.....

But back to this hike, questions remained about the next yellow, hairy guy. Was it a *Creeping Buttercup (Ranunculus repens)* whose flowers are golden yellow and glossy but the stems and leaves are finely hairy? Or was it a *Bulbous Buttercup (ranunculus bulbosus),* also known as St. Anthony's Turnip because of its bulbous underground stem? Perhaps my third guess is the charm: a *Hairy Cinquefoil (potentilla hirta)*. The answer will remain one of life's little mysteries until a real botanist comes along to set the record straight; may we all have such mundane questions to ponder in these challenging times!

Hairy Cinquefoil (potentilla hirta)

Still flanked by meadows on the trail, at least the next field of tall flowers were recognizable as belonging to the carrot family.

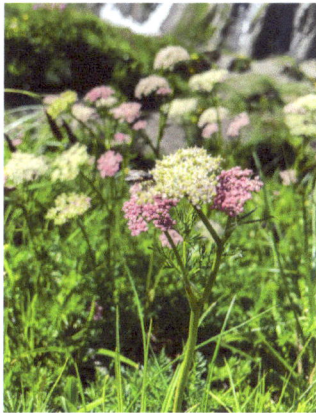

Greater Burnet Saxifrage (pimpinella major)

This ***Greater Burnet Saxifrage (pimpinella***

major) was branched and leafy. Very distinctive for having white and pink colored flowers on the same stem. Native to central Europe, it was very pretty.

Panorama looking down the trail we just hiked

We hiked circumnavigated a ridge which afforded a fantastic view of where we had started hours previously.

More Spring Gentians

More Spring Gentians lined the path and although they are related to a cousin, the Snow Gentian (gentiana nivalis), their stem structure is dissimilar. But their deep blue color is so mesmerizing…

So, let me introduce the next flower we saw on the TMB, the ***Kidney Vetch (anthyllis vulneraria)***. We had seen a few of these on previous hikes, but not as well formed and prolific.

Kidney Vetch (anthyllis vulneraria)

Kidney Vetch is well known for its medical uses (and vulneraria means "wound healer") both external and internal. It was introduced to Canada and the U.S. but is native to Europe.

The Pyramidal Bugle introduced in Chapter 2 that had bright pink flowers nestled in hairy leaves made another surprise appearance. This time the flowers were a mixture of blue, white and purple….

Pyramidal Bugle close up

We also saw a short evergreen shrub with lovely looking bell-shaped white flowers appearing in clusters. The flowers of **Cowberry (vaccinium vitis-idaea)** are followed by red, edible berries.

Cowberry (vaccinium vitis-idaea)

Also known as lingonberry, this is an important fruit crop for many northern regions of the world. Apparently they are a little bitter but can substitute for cranberries when cooked…

Those funky, pinkish Dr. Seuss-ish looking Mountain Houseleek flowers were back on the trail before we came across another type of rampion. The **Round-headed Rampion (phyteuma orbiculare)** is native to Europe, from the Pyrenees to the Balkans.

Round-headed Rampion (phyteuma orbiculare)

This striking, spiky flower is not a single bloom; if you look closely, the petals form small tubes that open at the top so that each plant sports 15-30 flowers! All websites state that the Round-headed Rampion is a "deep" or "sharp-blue, almost purple" wildflower, but it sure looks purple to me.

Here's an interesting vignette about the Round-headed Rampion: it's also known as the ***Pride of Sussex*** (as in the county of Sussex, England). As early as 1906, an author by the name of Frederick Gaspard Brabant wrote a book entitled "Sussex" in which he wrote,

> "the most beautiful flower on the chalk is the Round-headed Rampion (phyteuma orbiculara), locally called the 'Pride of Sussex'."

A quick google search describes the chalk cliffs of Sussex, made from pure white limestone formed from the remains of plankton at least 70 million years ago. Brabant must have been an incredible hiker as he published other books entitled: "Rambles in Sussex" (1909), "The English Lakes "(1902) and "Snowdonia" (year?), the latter about the region around the highest mountain in Wales (Snowdon). I couldn't find any biographical information about F.G. Brabant, but what a formidable rambler he must have been!

SIDEBAR to the day's hike: there's no nice way to say this……without variants and only one trail, there were hordes of people on this day, especially sprawled out all over the Col eating lunch.

Signage for Grand Col Ferret

Yes, the views were spectacular and the flowers omnipresent, but if you're looking for a "Sound of Music" moment, just know that won't happen on well publicized hiking trails. Looking at the bright side, hiking over the **Grand Col Ferret** meant that our feet had had taken us from Italy into Switzerland and that was an accomplishment to be celebrated.

Swiss Chalet in Ferret

Hours after leaving the Col, we were outside of **Ferret** (where we would catch a bus to Champex) and it was quite obvious that we were, indeed, in Switzerland!

CHAMPEX TO TRIENT

A fter a fantastic overnight stay at a family owned, picture-perfect chateau in Switzerland (featuring a home-cooked dinner with fresh vegetables from their garden), we set off the next morning as a group with two different agendas.

Lac de Champex

We all walked around the very scenic **Lac de Champex** and followed a bunch of confusing trails in the woods leading to a road where the trail would split in two: the regular TMB **Alp Bovine** and the much higher, arduous **Fenêtre d'Arpette** route. Both routes would eventually bring us down to the valley floor and the small village of **Trient** (160 permanent residents).

Not knowing what the snow conditions were on the higher variant, and fresh from remembering our rescue on Day 2 by the Swedish snow angel Andreas, I was in risk adverse mode. Paul talked a few of our friends into following him while I opted for the official (and safe!) route that went via Alp Bovine, touted in the brochure as "a splendid walk through pine and larch forests interspersed with alpine meadows and wonderful views down the Rhône Valley." Other than a few miles here and there, I'd be spending the whole day hiking with various members of our group.

I had fun pointing out flowers that I had already identified thanks to the book bought in Courmayeur. We saw Bearded Bellflowers that soon gave way to waves of gorgeous pink ***Alpine Bistort (bistorta vivipara)*** that were tall and willowy on the banks of a mountain stream.

Alpine Bistort (bistorta vivipara)

This bistort has a cousin in Colorado: a high-altitude, white variety found abundantly with other wildflowers. Our white bistorts contribute greatly to meadow mixes of purple, yellow, orange and red flowers. I was delighted to see, for the first time, a bright pink bistort!

Then we came across an unusual flower that took me many months to identify: a single spike with opposing purple flowers attached to the stem by the most unusual brackets. As a native wildflower of Europe, as well as Western Asia and Northern Africa, this ***Meadow Clary (salvia pratensis)*** is in the mint family (as are common herbs we all know such as basil, sage, lavender, etc.).

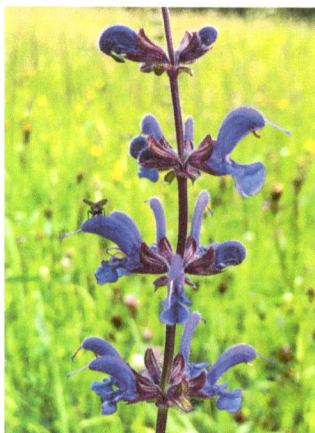

Meadow Clary (salvia pratensis)

A google search says that it's invasive in Washington State: not sure how it got there from Europe. And I had misidentified it for months (based on someone's European hiking blog) thinking that it was a Hedge Woundwort (stachys sylvatica) which is also in the mint family. Long story short: they are quite distinct. Look closer at this picture…I don't know exactly what pollinator was on the left petal of this Meadow Clary, but you can actually see the veins on its wings.

Speaking of pollinators, I wouldn't normally post two pictures of the same flower, but this ***Devil's Bit Scabious (succisa pratensis)*** is very photogenic with its tubular, purple flowers.

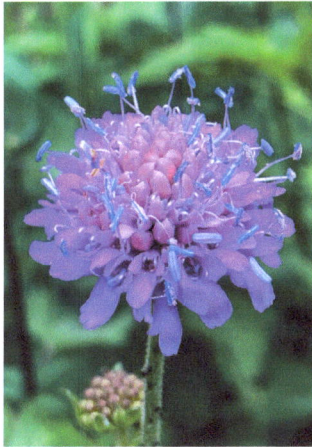

Devil's Bit Scabious (succisa pratensis)

And then a butterfly landed on one of them and I actually got a picture of it up close and in focus, amazing….

The Devil's Bit is a nectar-rich and common plant found throughout Europe, including the British Isles (but also having been introduced to parts of North America). The name

Butterfly on Devil's Bit Scabious

scabious is derived from the skin disease scabies (caused by a type of burrowing mite, ICK!); various species of this flower were supposed to help cure skin ailments, including sores caused by the bubonic plague. The Latin word for scratch is "scabere," hence "scabies." And the Devil's Bit portion of the flower name has to do with a legend that the devil was angry at the plant's medicinal properties so he tried to get rid of it by biting the roots off. So interesting to know there are stories and folklore while trekking through these beautiful trails that have existed for centuries!

Alpine Sowthistle (cicerbita alpina)

Somewhere on the trail we came across an ***Alpine Sowthistle (cicerbita alpina),*** an unremarkable looking plant that I took little notice of and, only months later, decided to add it to this list of TMB wildflowers.

Perhaps I was a little jaded after five days of fabulous wildflower surprises on the trail, but after researching this plant, it is definitely worthwhile to note that we saw it (field research!). The Alpine Sowthistle is native to European mountains, from the Alps to northern Scandinavia, and is actually endangered in Scotland. In Finland, bears, reindeer and elk feed on it, so it has a role in the European eco-system.

Ok, here's a repeat of a flower from Chapter 2, the Self-Heal (prunella vulgaris). The earlier one was light purple; today's flower was dark purple and the flowers, being "two-lipped and tubular," were fascinating.

Another Self-Heal

The fine hairs on this plant makes the Self-Heal worthy of close up inspection. And get this: it's an edible herb containing vitamins A, C and K that is used in salads and soups. Remember the quote at the beginning of this book? *"If you look the right way, you can see that the whole world is a garden."*

Keeping that quote in mind, the next flowers found on the trail was a thriving clump of **Wild Thyme (thymus serpyllum)**, happily camped out on a rocky outcrop.

Wild Thyme (thymus serpyllum)

Wild thyme is native to the "palearctic" zone of Europe and Asia; butterflies and bees find it most attractive. This variety is rarely used in cooking but is used as a groundcover in many gardens. Wild Thyme's medicinal uses are widely known both for its antiseptic properties and its beneficial effect on the digestive system. Keep an eye out for it in stores that carry products made of essential oils and herbs.

More Alpine Red Campions

OK, I can't resist adding another picture of Alpine Red Campions (silene dioica), a flower we saw on Day 1; not only is it an attractive, bright pink flower, but it seemed to be omnipresent on so many trails....

Yes, this is a book entirely about the *flora* of the Tour du Mont Blanc, but now a quick word about the iconic, world-famous Swiss *fauna*. Not the remote, rock-hopping ibex of folklore fame, but the family-owned, domesticated and picturesque bovines that dot the landscape. Listening to clanging cowbells and watching multi-colored cows serenely chewing on what I can only hope was delicious pasture grass is really as fun as all the tourist brochures make it out to be.

The Alp Bovine route has several locations where you need to close meadow gates or take care not to touch an electric fence. I know that different breeds of Swiss cows produce milk for particular types of cheeses but, being totally ignorant in that department, I focused on enjoying the music produced from the enormous bells hanging around their necks!

Bucolic cows along the TMB

More Common (Pink) Sainfoin

As we were hiking down a very steep path that led to the little town of **Trient**, the trail was lined with pink sainfoins (seen previously) but it also included a new flower.

This ***Blue Echium (echium vulgare)***, also known as viper's bugloss or blueweed, was very tall (like 3 feet) with single stem spikes.

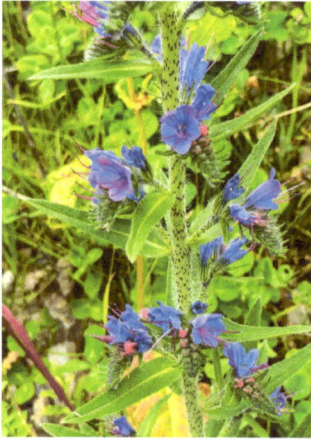

Blue Echium (echium vulgare)

The flowers start off as pink and turn vivid blue, almost purple, with prominent protruding red stamens. It is native to Europe and some parts of Asia; it has been introduced to North America as well as Chile. Many gardeners cultivate it as an ornamental plant. I have to admit that I overlooked this flower until months after I had returned to Colorado and was reviewing pictures from the TMB. Long after the hike was finished, I kept finding surprises and rewards amongst the hundreds of pictures I had taken!

Impressively tall Blue Echium

TRIENT - COL DE BALME - CHAMONIX

Our last night's accommodation on TMB in Trient was quite a letdown after the previous night's stay at a picturesque, family run chalet in Champex. As our group was split into two hotels, my assigned hostel was packed to the gills with backpackers and featured overflowing communal bathrooms (literally water running out onto the hallways), a private room the size of a shoebox and a marginal fondue dinner that made us nostalgic for all the homemade food we were served the night before.

But the walk out of Trient the next morning was worth a bad night's sleep! Passing by the iconic **pink church of Trient** was a 'postcard' moment, one of the most beautiful snapshots of the entire hike.

Famous Pink Church in Trient

After departing Trient, we spent the next few hours hiking to the French border at the **Col de Balme**, elevation 2,195 m (7,188 ft). There were a few Great Masterworts along the way, but not much else in the wildflower department.

We arrived at the **Refuge du Col de Balme** early and, as lunch wasn't served until noon, we stopped in to warm up, eat a few snacks, then head off in the direction of Le Tour via the GR Tour du Mont Blanc.

Refuge du Col de Balme

As we descended, the views were spectacular in all directions. The **Mont Blanc Massif** was coming into focus, including the summit of Mont Blanc, the Aiguilles, the Mer de Glace and the Argentière glaciers! As we dropped into lush meadows, flower surprises sprang forth to add color and intrigue to an already jaw-dropping hike.

Hiking towards the Chamonix Valley

Small White Orchid (pseudorchis albida)

A light green, singular stem with clusters of white, bell-shaped flowers caught my eye. At the time, I thought it was a lily of some kind, but it wasn't until months later that I identified it as a ***Small White Orchid (pseudorchis albida)***.

It's worthy of two pictures here, one that includes the leaf structure and one that shows the delicate flowers.

Small White Orchid

Although it is found in the Alps, Scandinavia, Greenland and the Russian mountains (such as the Urals), apparently it becomes quite rare the farther north you travel.

There are websites that describe how difficult it is to find the Small White Orchid in both Ireland and Finland; it is completely protected by law in both countries. In eastern Canada, it's known as the "Newfoundland Orchid," extending into polar latitudes and considered vulnerable because of its limited distribution and "low numbers" of occurrence. A Finnish website postulates that, because it's only found in one location on the other side of the Atlantic, ***the plant probably trav-***

eled there with the Vikings! And get this, the Small White Orchid is the *only member* of the genus Pseudorchis.

Bladder Campions above Mont Blanc Massif

Trekking through high meadows above the valley, we were greeted by various wildflowers we had seen previously. And with the Mont Blanc Massif in the background, the flowers in the foreground took center stage, including a tall, willowy grouping of white, Bladder Campions.

Butter-yellow Globeflowers (Bouton d'Or as you remember from Chapters 4 & 5) made a spectacular appearance as they swayed delicately in the breeze and, yes, this was definitely a "Sound of Music" moment.

Globeflowers and Book Cover

The above photo just says so much about hiking the Tour du Mont Blanc: the gorgeous scenery, an iconic wildflower, the lushness of green meadows, blue skies and monumental mountains. It was an obvious choice for the cover of this book….

As we continued our journey towards the Chamonix Valley, the trail was lined by the ever lovely, shocking pink Alpenrose. Other favorites from previous days such as Scheuchzer's Bellflower and Spiked Rampions graced the meadow scene as well.

Alpenrose framing the Mont Blanc Massif

Unusual and more rare flowers began to pop up. The Early Purple Orchids that we had seen on Day 1 were found again amongst grassy clusters. And a small purple flower I had not photographed before was located nearby.....

Carpet Bugle (ajuga reptans)

This ***Carpet Bugle (ajuga reptans)*** is a herbaceous flowering plant in the mint family and is native to Europe.

And then, joy of joys! A few Black Vanilla Orchids were found in nearby grasses though none of them were as photogenic as the ones found on Day 3.

Walking down the steep hillside to **Le Tour** (where we

would catch the bus to Chamonix), we looked up to notice that the upper hillside was dotted with amazing tall stalks of white lilies.

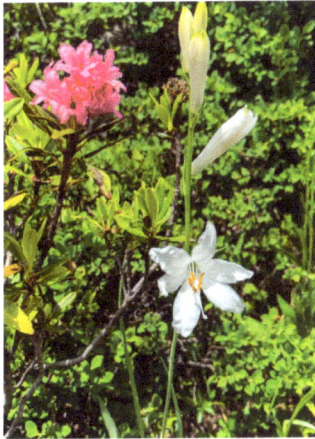

St Bruno's Lily (paradisea liliastrum)

I've seen very tall Washington Lilies in Oregon that have repopulated disturbed areas but I don't remember seeing any flowers like these in Colorado. As this was the first and only time we saw them on the TMB, I was very intrigued.

Later, I would figure out they were ***St. Bruno's Lily (paradisea liliastrum),*** native to the alpine meadows of southern Europe. And, believe it or not, this lily is a genus of flowering plants in the Asparagus family! These pure white flowers are as big as your open hand and sport very prominent bright orange anthers.

St. Bruno's Lily

Their history is fascinating as well: the name St. Bruno's Lily refers to a founder of Carthusian order of monks in the 11th century; his "motherhouse" was in the French Alps, where this plant can be found.

One last discovery was yet to be revealed before we dropped down into the ski resort of Le Tour to wait for the bus to Chamonix. I have only one picture of this flower: it's a ***Betony-Leaved Rampion (phyteuma betonici-folium Vill)*** which is related to but different than the Spiked Rampions and the Round-headed Rampions found on earlier hikes.

What little history can be gleaned about this flower relates to a fascinating botanist from the 18th century whose name was **Domínque Villars**. His great work was entitled ***The History of the Delfinado Plants*** (published from 1786 to 1789) and was based upon 20 years of observations. This book described over 2,700 species, including the betany-leaved rampion!

Betony-Leaved Rampion (phyteuma betonicifolium Vill)

In this day and age can you believe that anyone would spend so much time on such an endeavor? His herbarium and botanical manuscripts are preserved in the **Natural History Museum of Grenoble**; I'm hoping that some enterprising graduate student either has written, or plans to write, a thesis that would compare Villars's specimens from centuries ago to what we see in the field today....

Returning to the city of Chamonix was a juxtaposition of natural and artificial worlds. The bus from Le Tour dropped us off right at the plaza where the Climbing World Cup 2019 competition was being held.

Climbing World Cup 2019 Competition in Chamonix

Two specially built climbing walls, a big screen and 20 exhibitors (including beer booths!) captivated the attention of hundreds of spectators as they watched lead and speed climbers from around the world.

We sat down on the **Place du Mont Blanc**, took off our daypacks, boots and socks, bought and quaffed a few beers and faded into the surrounding tourism scene.

The walk to the hotel was spectacular but bittersweet: a great end to a great week of hiking!

Arve River in beautiful downtown Chamonix

ACKNOWLEDGMENTS

When our good buddy Geoff Wainwright informed us that he and John Hadley were organizing a group of friends to hike the Tour du Mont Blanc in the summer of 2019, my husband and I let Geoff know that we were "all in!" I had researched the TMB several years earlier and decided that making individual reservations looked daunting.

Geoff and John selected the UK based tour operator Macs Adventure for our self-guided tours (we could choose 7-8 days or 12 days) and within weeks of sending out the information, dozens of their friends had signed up for this incredible adventure! **Kudos to Geoff and John** for handling the myriad of details, communications, emails, logistics, etc., etc., that went into making this trip a reality. And apologies to members of our group as they may have only seen Paul and me at dinner or breakfast as we were on a mission: to hike variants off the main TMB and, in my case, seek out wildflowers along the way.

I'd also like to thank **Nicole Brès**, a friend of ours who lives in Paris, for her assistance in identifying various wildflowers in this book. She also suggested using the app PlantNet that was extremely helpful.

And last but not least, ***our fragile planet is being loved to death***: between climate change and vastly increasing numbers of people traveling to ever more distant locations, you are called to action. Be a citizen scientist and help preserve and document existing flora and fauna; practice leave-no-trace hiking and backpacking; carbon off-set your travels; and give generously to organizations that are making a difference. There are many ways to help save the planet and the many eco-systems that have endured for tens of millions of years. ***Get involved***!

TMB Trekkers July 2019
14 Day Trip
Kristin Biggins; Anne Inoue & Tom Lem; Hillary Brick; Phil Klass; Dan Houk; Jean-Michel (JM) & Sheri Maarek, Rafael, Jacob, Alitza; Jon Houk; Geoff Wainwright & Eda van Dyk

8 Day Trip
Mike Baldwin & Carol Takata; Paul Kluck & Leslie Madsen; Elizabeth (Betsy) Watson; Carolyn & Randy Bumatay; Ralph Reschke & Eradio Beltran; Lynne Conners; Mort, Susan & Kim Rowgheni; John (JD) Donaldson & Nina Corson; Herb & Carin Lim; John Hadley & Kathy Standen; Sam Toh & Kathy Loo

7 Day Trip
Jeff & Leslie Gold

APPENDIX OF WILDFLOWERS

Chapter 1

- Bearded Bellflower (campanula barbata)
- Scheuchzer's Bellflower (campanula scheuchzeri)
- Martagon Lily (lilium martagon)
- Common Spotted Orchid (dactylorhiza fushii)
- Early Purple Orchid (orchis mascula)
- Alpine Red Campion (silene dioica)
- Bladder Campion (silene vulgaris)
- Water Avens (geum rivale)
- Goatsbeard Spiraea (aruncus diocus)
- Great Masterwort (astrantia major)
- Greater Knapweed (centaurea scabiosa)
- Field Scabious (knautia arvensis)
- Red Trefoil (trifolium rubens)
- Spotted Longhorns (rutpela maculate) beetles!

Chapter 2

- Great Yellow Gentian (gentiana lutea)
- Hoary Plantain (plantago media)
- Wig Knapweed (centaurea phrygia subsp. psedophrygia)
- Bird's Foot Trefoil (lotus alpinus)
- Imperforate St. John's Wort (hypericum maculatum crantz)
- Common Hedgenettle (stachys officinalis)
- Dark Rampion (phyteuma ovatum)
- Common Sainfoin (onobrychis vicifolia)
- Self-Heal (prunella vulgaris)
- Matted Globularia (globularia cordifolia)
- Golden Hawksbeard (crepis aurea)
- Nottingham Catchfly (silene nutans)
- Mountain Houseleek (sempervivum montanum)
- Yellow Bellflower (campanula thyrsoides)
- Alpine Pasqueflower (pulsatilla alpine apiifolia)
- Alpine Forget-Me-Not (myosotis alpestris)
- Pyramidal Bugle (ajuga pyramidalis)

Chapter 3

- Least Primrose (primula minima)
- Spring Gentian (gentiana verna)
- Alpine Snowbell (soldanella alpina)
- Yellow Whitlow-Grass (draba aizoides)
- Glacier Crowfoot (ranunculus glacialis)
- Round-leaved Pennycress (noccaea rotundifolia)
- Creeping Avens (geum reptans)
- Moss Campion (silene acaulis)
- Trumpet Gentian (gentiana acaulis)
- Black Vanilla Orchid (gymnadenia rhellicani)
- Recurved Sandwort (minuartia recurva)

- Mountain Thrift (armeria alpina)
- White Pasqueflower (pulsatilla vulgaris 'alba')
- Spotted Gentian (gentiana puntata)
- Alpenrose (rhododendron ferrugineum)
- Buckler Mustard (biscutella laevigata)
- Wood Cranesbill (geranium sylvaticum)
- Adenostyles (adenostyles alliariae)

Chapter 4

- Bouton d'Or Poster
- Saussurea Alpine Botanical Garden
- Edelweiss (leontopodium nivale)

Chapter 5

- Wolfsbane (aconitum lycoctonum)
- Globeflower (trollius europaeus)
- Alpine Avens (geum montanum)
- Hairy Cinquefoil (potentilla hirta)
- Greater Burnet Saxifrage (pimpinella major)
- Spring Gentian (gentiana verna) repeat!
- Kidney Vetch (anthyllis vulneraria)
- Cowberry (vaccinium vitis-idaea)
- Round-headed Rampion (phyteuma orbiculare)

Chapter 6

- Alpine Bistort (bistorta vivipara)
- Meadow Clary (salvia pratensis)
- Devil's Bit Scabious (succisa pratensis)
- Alpine Sowthistle (cicerbita alpina)
- Self-Heal (prunella vulgaris) repeat!
- Wild Thyme (thymus serpyllum)

- Alpine Red Campion (silene dioica) repeat!
- Blue Echium (echium vulgare)

Chapter 7

- Small White Orchid (pseudorchis albida)
- Bladder Campion (silene vulgaris) repeat!
- Globeflower (trollius europaeus) repeat!
- Alpenrose (rhododendron ferrugineum) repeat!
- Carpet Bugle (ajuga reptans)
- St. Bruno's Lily (paradisea liliastrum)
- Betony-Leaved Rampion (phyteuma betonicifolium Vill)

ABOUT THE AUTHOR

Leslie Madsen lives in Denver, Colorado, and spends her summers hiking in the Rocky Mountains. She's also hiked the Overland Track in Tasmania, the Milford Track in New Zealand and the Laugavegur in Iceland. She's heli-hiked in Canada (luxury!) and has organized many independent hikes for herself (and husband Paul) that include Slovenia (the Julian and Kamnik Alps), hut trips in the Dolomites as well as hiking the entire Amalfi Coast (from Amalfi-Praiano-Positano-Sorrento). Her account of hiking the W Circuit in Patagonia (twice!) is entitled "Torres del Paine: A Tale of Two Trips" and is available through the Kindle store on Amazon.

Always a fan of flowers, it's only been the last few years that she's spent time documenting wildflowers she finds while hiking. Madsen believes that amateur photographers are now citizen scientists as the collision forces of climate change and overpopulation are changing the landscapes faster than any of us could have predicted.

Her photos have been featured in coffeeshops in Denver and in bookstores in Boulder County.

Madsen received a Masters of Arts degree from the University of Denver; in a prior life she worked as an international trade specialist for the Governor's Office and the international marketing manager for Denver International Airport. Although hiking is her number one activity, in the winter she enjoys skiing (downhill and cross country) and leading snowshoe trips. When not hiking in the summer, she plays tennis, rides bikes and swims like a tortoise!

For more photos and updates:
www.wildfloweraficionado.com

Picture of author and husband Paul on Col de la Seigne

www.ingramcontent.com/pod-product-compliance
Lightning Source LLC
Chambersburg PA
CBHW042131040426
42336CB00036B/4